The First Noel

The First Noel

Illustrated by Jody Wheeler

Ideals Children's Books • Nashville, Tennessee

Published by Ideals Publishing Corporation
Nashville, Tennessee 37214

Printed and bound in Mexico.

Library of Congress Cataloging-in-Publication Data
Wheeler, Jody.
The first noel/illustrated by Jody Wheeler.
p.   cm.
Summary: Illustrates the well-known carol in which an angel
appears to poor shepherds to announce the birth of Christ.
ISBN 0-8249-8565-6
1. Carols, English—Text. 2. Christmas music. [1. Carols.
2. Christmas music.] I. Title.
PZ8.3.W566Fi   1992   92-14438   CIP   AC

The illustrations in this book were rendered in watercolor paints.
The display type was set in Shelley Allegro.
The text type was set in Caslon 540.
Color separations were made by Stroud Graphics.

For Vanessa and Julien.
— J.W.

The first Noel the angel did say
was to certain poor shepherds in fields
    as they lay,
in fields where they lay keeping their sheep
on a cold winter's night that was so deep.

They looked up and saw a star
shining in the east, beyond them far.
And to the earth it gave great light,
and so it continued both day and night.

And by the light of that same star,
three wise men came from country far.

To seek for a king was their intent
and to follow the star wherever it went.

This star drew nigh to the northwest;
o'er Bethlehem it took its rest.
And there it did both stop and stay,
right over the place where Jesus lay.

Then did they know assuredly
within that house the king did lie;
one entered it them for to see
and found the babe in poverty.

Then entered in those wise men three,
full reverently upon the knee,
and offered there, in his presence,
their gold and myrrh and frankincense.

$\mathcal{B}$etween an ox stall and an ass,
this child truly there he was;

for want of clothing they did him lay
All in the manger, among the hay.

Noel, noel, noel, noel
Born is the king of Israel.

The First Noel

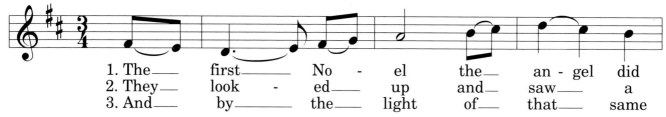

1. The first No - el the an - gel did
2. They look - ed up and saw a
3. And by the light of that same

say Was to cer - tain poor shep - herds in
star Shin - ing in the east, be -
star, Three wise men came from

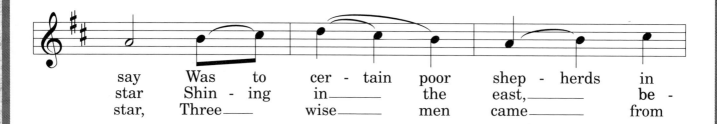

fields as they lay; In fields where
yond them lay far. And fields to the
coun - try far. To seek for a

they lay keep - ing their sheep On a
earth it gave great light, And
king was their in - tent And to

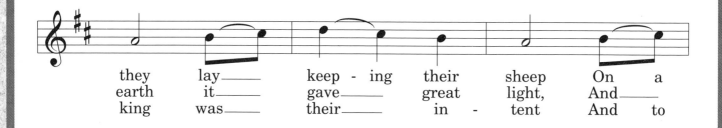

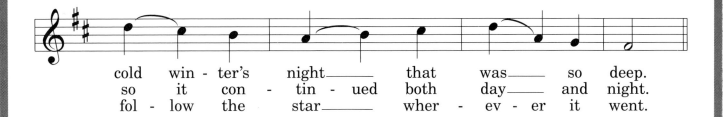

cold   win - ter's   night_____   that   was_____   so   deep.
so   it   con - tin - ued   both   day_____   and   night.
fol - low   the   star_____   wher - ev - er   it   went.

No - el,_____   no - el,   no - el,   no - el.

Born   is   the   king_____   of   Is - ra - el.

4. This star drew nigh to the northwest;
   O'er Bethlehem it took its rest.
   And there it did both stop and stay,
   Right over the place where Jesus lay.

5. Then did they know assuredly
   Within that house the king did lie;
   One entered it them for to see
   And found the babe in poverty.

6. Then entered in those wise men three,
   Full reverently upon the knee
   And offered there, in his presence,
   Their gold and myrrh and frankincense.

7. Between an ox stall and an ass,
   This child truly there he was;
   For want of clothing they did him lay
   All in the manger, among the hay.

The First Noel

The First Noel first appeared in print in 1833, but it was handed down for many generations before it was published. It is thought that this carol was popular in seventeenth-century England, when church leaders did not allow their congregations to sing—only trained choirs could sing inside the church. The choirs' songs were most often somber chants with little melody.

Church-goers took their singing voices outside, where they were joined by wandering minstrels who provided music. Together, they created joyful carols, like *The First Noel*, and they made up circle dances to perform with the songs. At that time, the English word "carol" actually meant "a ring or circle dance." As time passed, "carol" came to refer to the song, rather than to the dance.

Historians cannot agree whether *The First Noel* originated in France or England because the French word *noel* and English word *nowell* sound identical, and their long-ago meanings are not clear. Today, these two words mean exactly the same thing—a Christmas carol.